Leaves of Peace
An Anthology of Poetry

First Edition, June 2020

ISBN: 979-8644804252

Leaves of Peace Editor:
Jan Chronister

Leaves of Peace Associate Editor:
Lucy Tyrrell

Leaves of Peace Editorial Committee:
Naomi Cochran, Sara Sarna

Cover: *Paper Birch with New Spring Leaves*
Photograph by Lucy Tyrrell

Additional copies can be purchased from
peaceanthology@gmail.com or Amazon.com

About *Leaves of Peace*

In March 2019, June G. Paul of Portage, Wisconsin began collecting poems about peace for a project that eventually became "Tree of Peace." June formatted the poems on a maple leaf template with the idea of displaying them at various poetry events around the state, including Wisconsin Fellowship of Poets (WFOP) conferences. Jan Chronister approached June with the idea of collecting a selection of these poems in an anthology to commemorate International Day of Peace (September 21) with readings around Wisconsin.

From the Editors

As the project moved forward, and the deadline for poem submissions neared (March 30, 2020), it was obvious that our country was in a serious situation. Some of the poems submitted later in the submission period reflect this reality, but this *Leaves of Peace* anthology was never intended to focus on the pandemic. Instead, it offers peace and comfort through the poems themselves. Often this peace is found in nature. Some poems are angry, some look back at history, and some look forward to a better time, but they all confirm the power of poetry to express what often cannot be said in any other way.

None of us expected to be where we are today. It is our hope that this anthology will strengthen the community of Wisconsin poets and bring us closer together in a time when we must stay apart.

Thanks to everyone who trusted us with their work. Over 100 poems were submitted from well-known poets as well as from those whose names were new to us. Our selection was "blind." There were some discussions, but we agreed on the collection you hold in your hands.

Thanks to June G. Paul for her vision and dedication to the project. Thanks to Wisconsin Fellowship of Poets for the grant that made the printing of this anthology possible.

iv

Leaves of Peace is dedicated to Ellen Kort,
Wisconsin's First Poet Laureate (2000 – 2004),
for her commitment to peace and poetry.

Contents

vi

Ellen Kort

Peace

Oh the swell of it
December's white room of snow
the moon's round slice of silence
random stars dazzling the sky
Peace
keep moving   keep singing from
branch to house to door   unravel
the knots   whisper the breath line
of love   weave us together
Peace
keep us wakeful in dark places
polish the compass of compassion
beating in our heart   teach us
to follow the north star   to forgive
to reach out   to be humbly amazed

Ellen Kort

Unity Tree

Let us circle the tree   let it
Rise Bless the strength
of its roots its wings of song
the way it wears the stunning
light of morning   Let it be
a lamp for peace a prayer wheel
where love circles and multiplies
Let it be an altar a resting place
where we can tell one another
all the stories of the world

first published in *The Sacred Grove: Spreading Seeds of Peace*

Janine Arseneau

Practicing Peace

For peace is a practice too
as much as tai chi or yoga
kickboxing or meditation

It does not arrive full born
or well understood.
It comes unfinished
ready to be experienced

      A scrap of origami
      collapses on itself
      patterns overlaying patterns

Unfold it gently
over time
in the limned light of soft patience
with the courage of great care

Mary Jo Balistreri

Finding Peace

To walk these meandering paths
of filtered sun and fallen birch logs
is to inhale peace.
To tread upon pine needles
cushioned with downy white tufts
of aspen calms even the most
anxious thoughts.
To surrender to the wind as does
the arboreal forest brings solace.
To rest awhile on glacier stone, see
trilliums commingle with oaks
and bursts of bright yellow Lady's slippers
fills your heart to overflowing.
To hear a hermit thrush sing praise,
its melody scented with pine
is to know the god within.
To stay awhile and deep breathe
honors the sacredness we each carry.

first published on *Wilda Morris's Poetry Challenge blog*

Vlasta Karol Blaha

Not All Faces

I recall my mother's response
when I phoned to say I needed
white yarn to crochet my dolls' faces.
Not all faces are white, she said.

Now my four crocheted dolls,
two deep brown faces
two white yarn faces
their arms linked,
daydream together side by side
on my embroidered heirloom quilt.

My mother always envisioned
a world united in harmony,
all races together
smiling, holding hands—
our world at peace.

Sara Burr

A Peaceful Grief

I browse awhile.
My books are old
and so have I become. Still
a lonesome future lies before me.

My books are old
and greatly loved,
but a lonesome future lies before me;
our time cannot return.

And greatly loved,
you, as well
though our time cannot return
because your body's gone.

You as well
loved words that linger,
and while your body's gone
I still browse among our books.

You loved words that linger
and me as well. Today
your ghost has come
to browse with me awhile.

Jan Chronister

Finding Peace on Prince Edward Island

My great-great-grandfather stood
in his red coat
facing minutemen's muskets
across the Concord,
listened to "the shot heard round the world."

Losing an eye and leg
he was rewarded by King George
with land on "the gentle island"
across the bay from Summerside.

Two centuries later,
hoisted atop my dad's shoulders,
I see the young queen's train
pass by a cheering crowd in Canada.

The river today is so calm
a maple leaf tossed from shore
goes nowhere,
floating in a circular dance of peace.

Naomi Cochran

Small Change

The silent cross-shaped mouth
receives my coins, communion wafers
of the Salvation Army.
Do this in remembrance of me.

The kettle is chained,
unattended,
easily ignored.
When you give alms, give in secret.

My daughter's milk money
becomes another's food and shelter.
Do not be anxious for tomorrow,
for tomorrow will care for itself.

My pockets are empty;
there is nothing left for the blood-red abyss
of the other army.
Do not kill.

Ten million dollars an hour
to destroy another's food and shelter.
As much as possible,
live in peace with one another.

first published in *Verse Wisconsin*

Jody Murad Curley

Horicon Salvation

It was the sighing of the marsh grass
that saved me.

It was the singing of sun and cloud,
the ringing of sky
and space.

It was the chance to take a long view,
unobstructed by human hands.

It was the freedom to not listen
to anyone or anything
but crow and crane
and wind in creaking trees.

It was the absence of being needed,
except for duck and goose,
osprey and eagle,
heron and hawk,
all needing me to simply let them be.

It was the shimmering of light on water.
It was the patience of earth
that saved me.

It was the peace.

Alice Ellis

Remembering Vietnam on a Bus

A middle-aged vet propped in a wheelchair
locked in place by bus straps. Coming home
from selling a rain bucket of roses.
Compressed by the battle, the soldier
was plowed under by flashbacks
to be reborn as a flower child—
a bargain earned at a high price.
He salutes another vet bent over a cane
with "have a good one."

I glance at the felt patch on his left eye
hair cranked back in a scrappy ponytail
a plastic crate belted to his chair,
open suitcase of a post-Nam life.
A thin-tin mug hammered by coins
Stars-and-Stripes patriotism ready for duty.
He carries a new peace symbol
scribbled on his bucket—
"I love your smile."

Thirty years since the war
limbs of collateral damage still are twisted.
He calls out for the next stop.
The bus halts. The door folds open.
The vet rolls out on the disabled ramp,
fiber pole waving an agent-orange flag.

Yvette Viets Flaten

Meditation

A long walk alone in the rain
puddles grow, drips shower
sidewalks glisten. No voices,
no cars pass, gentle drum
of drops on umbrella.

Lap of lake water against
the hull, subtle curl and kiss,
a gentle lift and sink against
bosom of waves, silent swell
rising like easy breath.

Warmth of welcome rest
after all the world's work. Heady
and solemn, a dampening of care,
to drift away into the sure embrace
of the boundless peace of sleep.

Joan Giusto

Confliction Addiction

A rock thrown in anger.
Sticks and stones breaking bones.
Then bows and arrows pierce the air,
axes and swords litter killing fields.

Gun powder, flintlocks, and muskets,
Man-O-War with armed cannons,
then airplanes dropping nerve gas,
atom bombs, and napalm.

Small blue planet
turning red, hot war, Cold War,
then trade war, cyber war, endless.
Wouldn't peace rock?

Annette Langlois Grunseth

The Cup

Hold your hands
one inside the other
listen to steady rain
roll off the porch roof
smooth your anxious edges
hands cupped, sip
on songs of house finches
sleek music of cardinals
amid an afternoon shower.
Listen for guidance within
take shelter, weather-out feelings
lean a while
let peace reside
in the cup of your hand—
soak up the Spirit
who is steady
like the rain.

first published in similar form in *Blue Heron Review*

Karen Haley

Inner Peace

We speak of it
as inner and private
not knowing it
spreads
touches those who
on every side
lean against us

Without it
sides can press in
crumble
smother our core
drown and extinguish
our voice

Hold on to that
center
make it strong
like solid timber
it will keep you
whole

Susan Martell Huebner

What You Will Notice First
after Iain Lonie

the impact
the way the air hits
your body as you step
out the door the FULL STOP
of the world your car parked
and locked your plans at the curb
next to the recycle bins

next you might notice
the silence
the way air holds quiet cupped
in open palms an offering of chittering
birds wild with spring the earth
breathing crocuses and daffodils
you might stand still hearing the scuttle
of leaves dancing across asphalt
all distilling into vibration and hum
under the cathedral of sky

Note: Iain Lonie is an Australian poet who died in 1988.

Maryann Hurtt

Stew

I think if I chop enough
corn, potatoes, onion, carrots
into my favorite green pot
I might save the world

look how the carrots dig deep
then leap
into our held out hands
how big-eyed potatoes search
for hungry mouths
and those ears of corn
waiting to hear
sighs of full bellies
as onion tears softly
to be included

we are all in this stew together
the table big and round
I will hang the welcome sign

Deb Johnston

Whispers of Peace

We wish to walk on sand,
to view tumbled treasures.
> *Take what you need, but leave the rest.*
> *Share the trove of the commons.*

We came to rest near your shore,
cleanse away our haste.
> *Let my waves wash up to greet you,*
> *dissolving the rush.*

We are here to renew and refresh,
caressed by lake breezes.
> *Resent no more—be still for my views.*
> *They travel on the wind and through the waves.*

We are mesmerized by melting sunsets,
unable to look away.
> *Allow the glowing orb to calm your intentions,*
> *reclaim your kindness.*

We are humbled by the horizon
and the presence of nature.
> *Look around at everything you have—*
> *let gratitude flow.*

Meridel Kahl

Respite

Voices in the news
sneer
snarl
snipe
growl
about walls   wars
winners   losers

as late winter snow
falls soft and slow.

White stretches
along maple limbs
settles into crevices
of wild plum
gathers in tufts
on blue spruce—

clean, cold silence
for a world whirling
in hot noise.

Estella Lauter

Making Peace

Until an Oneida student told me,
I'd never heard the story
told for centuries before the Conquest
of how the Haudenosaunee Peacemaker
came through his own sorrow
to mediate pain and anger

replacing one man's mean reflection
in the water for soup on a stove
with his own serene countenance,
and counting another's grievances
on a string of perfect shells
until they could be borne.

Face to face, he met the ones
who undermined their towns
with fear and hatred.
Face to face, he taught his people
to meet in the Longhouse
until they reached consensus
for the good of their nations.

And in his wisdom he advised
that Clan Mothers should choose
and depose the Chiefs.
He knew that women
are the first and last
resort for Peace.

Sandra Lindow

Seventy Year Moon

Brilliant stars and a seventy year
moon, closer than seen in a lifetime,
is an intimate song floating above rooftops;
it sings descant to bare boughs of cottonwood,
true notes of an ancient promise
that the galaxy goes on beyond human catastrophe.
You, who stand in the shadows, come look:
Too much has happened to look away, you
must seek songs in yourselves or truth will
pass like battalions goose-stepping
in full dress parade, leaving the powerless, only
a scrap of confetti and a bone of contention;
hurry, for the first time, see.

Note: Reading the first word of each line forms an Issa haiku.

Debra Monthei Manske

Xi'an, China

"May your hands show mercy
and may your feet care for green earth."
(on a stone at Giant Wild Goose Pagoda, Xi'an, China)

Seek out what you may
cherish in your
neighbor, entwine your hands
to carry forward the work, show
an abundance of mercy
as together you build grace and
joy so great grandchildren may
receive from your
effort a place for their feet
removed from care
inheriting from you a home for
peace—a beautiful, green
always sacred earth.

CJ Muchhala

woman with flute

hover with the hummingbird
between rock & cloud

feel the wingbeats

the cacti blossoming
into silence

listen

first published online in *Voices on the Wind # 68*

C. L. Nehmer

Hunger
Bethel, New York, 1969

We fill up on America, her burnt
Texaco and wheat fields waving,
her pop cans and M-16s, her patch
denim and tambourines. We come free
in the mud, fill ourselves with mouthfuls
of skunk smoke and pond water, sun
our faces and pink parts below surface
until we're cold and night
gathers herself like a prayer shawl
around the yard lights of our campfires
and the rain begins and begins, the breath
of a faraway death on our necks. We are
a patchwork of lawn to the soldiers
in helicopters, our arms and legs not
our own, labyrinthed, dew-covered,
paper cones of nuts and sunflower seeds
swaddled in our palms like children.

Elizabeth Harmatys Park

Expectation

dawn pink sky
shimmers above
the band of grey trees
that stands unmoving,
reflected in the pink lake

quiet, early
morning light
brings an expectation
of peace to a hushed
and softer world

June G. Paul

Learn to Seek Peace

There is a seed of peace
planted in your soul.
Open your heart,
see it grow.

Peace knows who you are,
and where you are.

Peace will happen
when you know
yourself
inside and out.

Peace knows when you
are discontented—
whispers "Be still,
learn to seek peace."

Tend the seed of peace
in your soul, feel it grow
from inside, swelling,
until it flows out to the world.

Ann M. Penton

Disarmament Decree

From this year onward
the right to be armed at school
only applies to the desks.
Period.
Underscore.
Bold.
Forever and ever.
Amen.

Mary Louise Peters

Clear a Corner

Amid the swirl and fear,
clear a corner.
Sweep it clean and smooth.
Find something small from nature—
a stone, a shell, a balsam fir pine cone—
cradle it in the center of a simple saucer.
Light your biggest pillar.
Give it time to burn and drip.
Wrap your softest blanket
around your shoulders.
Get down low.
Sit on the floor, grounded and still.
Curl into your own warmth and tented calm.
Bring the sound of raindrops
to tap on the taut fabric of your mind.
Savor the safety.
Watch the flame.
Tend it as if it were a bonfire.
Let your eyes carry kindling and kindness.
Stare away cares.
Breathe and break like a wave on the shore.
Push and pile all that has fallen.
Return to yourself.
Watch the flame at its wick.
Stay as long as you'd like.
Then, blow out the flame.
Send whirls of smoke
outward and other-bound
to calm the world.

Too Much Room

there's too much room on the National Mall
room to stroll through monuments tall

room to wander grove and hill
and ponder space we've yet to fill

local revolution or global strife
there's too much marble marking lives

marble marking so much blood
so much evil, so little good
chop down the cherry trees
stop spreading lies

sell off the lots
so no more die
divest ourselves of bronze and stone
invest in peace away, at home
there's too much room on the National Mall
and we're much too eager to fill it all

Deborah Rasmussen

I Have an Appointment with My Congressman

to talk about preventing war against Iran
through legislation
he opposes
so how to begin?

Find common ground
the experts advise
which reminds me of P
my sworn enemy in sixth grade
who startled me one day
by falling in step
as we walked home from school
by chatting as though we were friends
and listening as I chatted back
a small surprise
that didn't change everything
but did change
something.

I hold that memory
as I meet this person in power who
I suspect
disagrees with me but
who was a kid once too—
who might walk over ground
we have in common.

Georgia Ressmeyer

What I Tell Myself

My soul is my own today.
It will not pass
in a handshake, a hug,

be dropped when I
rummage in pockets
for keys or cell phone.

I won't panic, be frantic,
lose what's left of my cool.
I'm as calm as a stone.

If an ice storm blooms
in my garden,
I'll sniff it.

Political battles won't
bait me to be livid, hateful.
Likewise, the news.

Today I am the soul of peace,
cultivating forgiveness,
compassion, wisdom.

My soul is not for sale,
it is not for lease.
Chaos, for now, has ceased.

Patricia McNamee Rosenberg

Election Night

He stood in the kitchen refusing to
attend high school that day.

A celebration in Chicago's Grant Park
was planned for when the polls closed.

Our boy insisted on taking an early train
for a spot on the lawn of victory.

We worried that if his hero lost,
it could trigger a race riot.

As if overhearing our little family drama,
she phoned us from her hospital bed...

My mother-in-law, a Holocaust survivor,
who had marched with King,
had postponed death to see this moment.

She demanded we shelve our fears so her grandson
would be her surrogate in witnessing history.

She said, "Risk is the price we pay for peace."

Sara Sarna

this peace

It's a beautiful evening
and I don't want it to end.
If only they were all like this.
Not too hot or humid,
the mosquitoes on sabbatical,
some traffic sounds,
but mostly chirping insects and birds,
a lawnmower and a dog or two,
the breeze making the leaves
softly click and whisper.
Endless expanse of blue overhead
and a profusion of Queen Anne's lace
by my side.
I want to take a piece of this perfection
and tuck it away
in case something terrible happens
and we never have another moment like this.
Then I will take it out
when the world is dark
and share it,
tell stories that begin "I remember,"
because I've saved this piece—
this peace.

Jo Scheder

Meditation, Mānoa

Twelve koi shimmer in calm eddies,
reflected onto louvered window panes.

The white scales of *taisho sanke* now silver
beside the cadmium of *aka bekko*,
deepened in the leftover glow of sunset.

The sun now a mere thumb-spot,
an afterimage indistinguishable from the *sumi*,
small black markings on the koi, hypnotic,
a hundred shadow suns floating, tranquil, here.

Note: Mānoa is a neighborhood in Honolulu. *Taisho sanke* and *aka bekko*, are types of koi. *Sumi* are dark spots on the koi.

first published in *Museletter*

Paula Schulz

Prayer for a Common Language
for Shuku in her fifth year

She walks beneath the jacaranda trees,
looks up to see the petal-printed sky
warm and mild and welcome as a breeze
in summer's surprising heat. She is wise

for one so small and she is learning how
letters work, their sounds, their shapes like branches
of this tree that writes its story wide. Now
a calling: strange-to-my-ears birdsong launches

itself into air—yet another
language the child and I may learn. Each day
the world speaks in many voices. Brothers,
sisters, each of us has something to say.

We grow as flowering trees, live here under
the same sun, taste the same air.
We can learn how to speak out the wonders
our eyes record, share our stories, share

our lives, brief as tissues, vibrant as blossoms.

first published in *Wisconsin Poets' Calendar*

Kent Shifferd

Peace Workers

Small brown nut, dry seed of peace
we plant in the stony ground, in grey clays of despair.
We who have come from that other land
where the blind stumble and lunge
through deserts they have made from hate and fear,
we who have emerged from the shroud of violence,
incurring the wrath of those yet bound,
hew at this difficult soil and tear the fingers of our souls
and plant the seed.

Expect no flower-laden tree of life,
no slender, fragrant stem,
but gnarled oak,
twisted and angular with thick, ribbed bark
to protect it from the hacking of the cynics.
Expect a tree so tough that often it seems dead.
Much of the time it is winter on this plantation.

But always a few leaves come back.
Slowly it reclaims land from the deserts of war,
boneyards of blasted children,
poisoned ecosystems of the heart.
It will shade and shelter grasses
in a small, expanding circle, mothering the soil
for the eventual blooming of the planet.

We stand around with our small tools.
Others will come to nurture this tree
when we are laid to rest under its branches.

Marshall Smith

Meditation in Cairo
for Dr. Ahmed Abdelsalam

Sitting by the Nile
a listless cloudy day
wind stirring in the leaves
my terrace plants shiver
as the call to prayer
echoes in the streets below
so little of what we do matters
so little of what we think true is
the Imam's voice cries
sings and broadcasts through our neighborhood
does he cry out for justice among men
it's a language I don't understand
carefully we listen to our world
carefully we collect the clues
I am lost in Cairo
I will eat my lunch of almonds and dried figs
sip my green tea
waiting for the sun to go down
there is nothing I need

Gail Sosinsky

Thirst

In hospital,
the severed child
tilts water
to the bomber's lips.

Elaine Strite

Apostle Doves

Twelve gray doves cloister in a spruce tree,
solemn as apostles, chests puffed out,
they pray in the still, cold air.

They sigh, their chants a pneumatic pump
that gently fills the vacuum of sound
in their arboreal chapel.

Doves sometimes perch on the feeder,
not to feed, but to occupy it—
defending their Jerusalem.

Other times they browse on the ground,
shoulder-to-shoulder with squirrels—red, gray, black—
and with finches and sparrows:
Love thy neighbor as thyself.

Doves blend with gray skies,
clatter their wings
as they flutter back to the spruce
to resume their devotions—
devout monks at vespers.

If only jays, crows, and geese
were as blessedly meek.

Thomas Thrun

Yes, I will hold . . .

Today I placed a prayer
not online but in my head
the old-fashioned way.
Given what is going on
I was not surprised
Heaven put me on hold
promising to take my prayer
in the order in which it was
received.
So I left a message.
I prayed for
a new kind of peace
one that passes all understanding
as I don't understand
why people still get shot
in the streets of Milwaukee
while the rest of the world is
trying so hard to *social distance* itself
from anything/anyone which/who
might be COVID-19/coronavirus
contaminated.
God, I'm not really asking why
please just give my heart
peace—
a peace that passes
my inability to understand
to even comprehend
what is happening to our/your world
what is happening to all of us.
Amen.

Elizabeth Tornes

Deer Story

for my father, Jim Tornes

I remember the story you told us
about the deer that wandered onto the property
wearing an orange ribbon around her neck,
as if someone meant to say, *don't shoot!*
You went into the cottage, grabbed a carrot—
she sidled up to you, nibbled it down.
In your time, you'd shot plenty of her kind.
But she became your pet, appearing in the evening
near the house, where you'd drop old apples
and withered carrots. After several days,
you were able to stroke her neck. One day
you festooned her with orange survey ribbons
crisscrossed around her belly, her legs,
and tied a double bow beneath her chin.
Amazing how still
she stood while you wrapped her
like a peace offering
for all the world to see.

first published in *Up North Lit*

Peggy Trojan

At the Ranch at Santa Maria

I sat in the sunshine
on the patio
deep in the peace of the hills
so still a group of deer
came not thirty feet away
to graze and rest
in the pasture.
A yellow butterfly landed
inches from my chair
and a gray bird pecked
leisurely at crumbs by my feet.
By not moving
I became an acceptable
part of their innocent world,
none of us a threat.

first published in *All That Matters*

Jenny Tumas

Meeting the View

Ground slopes
an incremental slide
towards Lake Superior.

Ancient shoreline tilts
while white pines,
maple and birch

remain erect
on their plumbline.
Lupine barely register

the sky's drift.
Neon flag marks
the property line.

On my navy blue cushion
I sit in the back of my heart,
inside the curve of my upper back

where border shifts and dissipates.
I am trying to stay inside my body
meeting the view.

Teaching Yoga

A contented heart
soothes a jumping mind.
In winter's darkness,
we inhale lilac.
In summer's heat,
we exhale
forest evergreen.
Coming together
we multiply,
enfolded in peace.

Lucy Tyrrell

I will fight no more forever
after Chief Joseph (1877)

The group circles in chairs in the library basement
to share poems to commemorate our U.S. wars.
In planning the event, he and I agree we must add
American Indian wars.

The last of these Indian wars was swept away
ten decades ago—quivers of an uneasy peace,
shot through with lingering injustices.

I suggest he read a list from Wikipedia.
He tapes the printout pages end to end,
rolls them into a scroll of sorrow.
When it is time, he stands, undoes the band, lets the papers
unfurl until the white sheets spill across the floor—
with a gasp from the group. Each line, a war.
He reads for 20 minutes—names, years, combatants—
to a stunned silence.

Navajo Wars, Pequot War, Tuscarora War, Chickasaw
Wars, Tecumseh's War, Creek War, Arikara War, Ute
Wars, Tule River War, Black Hawk's War, Red Cloud's
War, Comanche Campaign, Red River War, Great Sioux
War of 1876, Ghost Dance War, Crazy Snake Rebellion,
Bluff War, Posey War.

The list does not enumerate
each battle, tragedy, bloody massacre,
attacks against innocent villages
where chiefs sought peace for their people
huddled in blankets of hunger.

B. D. Vess

Gentle Defiance

Freshly fallen snow,
still and silent,
shimmers under the depths
of a looming nocturne.

Mysterious and radiant,
gentle in its defiance of a
cold and unforgiving darkness,

this peace,
this silken sheet of starlight,

glistens in crisp perfection.

About the Poets

Janine Arseneau (Milwaukee) is a founding member of Grandmothers Beyond Borders and Community Pie. She writes on backs of receipts, scraps of fabric, margins of newspapers, and in tiny books made with reclaimed materials.

Mary Jo Balistreri (Waukesha) feels like going forward for peace is the very best thing we could do in 2020. Submitting to this project was a first step. *www.maryjobalistreripoet.com*

Vlasta Karol Blaha (Colby) shared poetry with her elementary school students and friends for four decades. Recently, she has begun writing and appreciates the inspiration from her poetry groups.

Sara Burr (Madison) has published her poetry in *Verse Wisconsin, Bus Lines* (Madison Metro), *Ariel Anthology, Wisconsin Poets' Calendar (2017), The Midwest Review 4*, and *Southwestern American Literature.*

Jan Chronister (Maple) has poems in a variety of print and online publications. Her first full-length poetry collection *Caught between Coasts* was recognized as an Outstanding Book of Poetry by the Wisconsin Library Association. Jan is serving as president of Wisconsin Fellowship of Poets 2015 – 2021.

Naomi Cochran (Hayward) is the author of *Finding Ourselves in Alzheimer's, Fill in the Blank, Razed Lutheran,* and *The Truth About Everything—in 3500 Words or Less.* She serves as the membership chair for Wisconsin Fellowship of Poets.

Jody Murad Curley (Madison) is a poet, Tai Chi Chuan teacher, and ordained Universalist Sufi minister who lives as close to Cherokee Marsh as she can get.

Alice J. Ellis (Ashland) is a retired middle school language arts teacher. Alice and her husband are living on the family land in northern Wisconsin for their retirement years.

Yvette Viets Flaten (Eau Claire) loves languages and words and has had her poetry published widely. She and husband Dan enjoy summer travels, near and far.

Joan Giusto (Tomahawk) is a retired vagabond whose poetry and prose has appeared in several anthologies in the United States and Ireland.

Annette Langlois Grunseth (Green Bay) seeks peace and poetry through her muse and is a Pushcart Prize nominee for her chapbook *Becoming Trans-Parent: One Family's Journey of Gender Transition*. *www.annettegrunseth.com*

Karen Haley (Milwaukee) writes, hikes, paints, gardens, working hard to balance this quiet with the exuberance of her many grandchildren and their parents— not always successfully!

Susan Martell Huebner (Mukwonago) is the author of a literary novel *She Thought the Door was Locked* and a poetry chapbook *Reality Changes with the Willy Nilly Wind*. *www.susanmhuebner.com*

Maryann Hurtt (Elkhart Lake), now retired after thirty years of hospice nursing, continues to love stories of resiliency and wisdom in hard times. Aldrich Press published her chapbook *River* in 2016 and her poems have appeared in a variety of print and online publications.

Deb Johnston (Marshfield), a former educator, writes from central Wisconsin. Her work has appeared in Wisconsin Poets' Calendars, *Design Magazine*, The Education Center,® and *Poets to Come, a Walt Whitman Anthology*.

Meridel Kahl (Duluth, Minnesota) retired in 2013 after 45 years of teaching. She spent the last 27 years at The College of St. Scholastica in Duluth. Her great-great grandparents, immigrant farmers, settled in Prairie Farm, Wisconsin, a place dear to her heart.

Ellen Kort (Appleton) was Wisconsin's first Poet Laureate, serving from 2000 – 2004. Ellen passed away in 2015. During her rich life, she used her skills as a poet and teacher to reach out to the community in numerous ways, teaching at local universities and schools and conducting writing workshops for at-risk teens, nurses, physicians, and for survivors of cancer, AIDS, and domestic abuse. Ellen authored 11 books and 8 collections of poetry. Her work has been featured in a variety of anthologies and incorporated architecturally in downtown Milwaukee's Midwest Express Center, the Green Bay Botanical Gardens, and the Fox River Mall. Also, Ellen's poetry has been performed by the New York City Dance Theatre and recorded on audio by Ellen Burstyn, Ed Asner, and Alfre Woodard. She was a guest on Wisconsin Public Radio and National Public Radio and traveled widely as a poet, speaker, and poetry workshop facilitator throughout the U.S., New Zealand, Australia, the Bahamas, and Japan. The Ellen Kort Peace Park in Appleton is in the planning stages.

Estella Lauter (Fish Creek) has published four chapbooks with Finishing Line Press and received two Pushcart nominations. As Poet Laureate of Door County in 2013 – 2015, she founded the Door County Poets Collective to publish *Soundings: Door County in Poetry*. She co-edited the 2017 *Wisconsin Poets' Calendar* with Francha Barnard on the theme of water.

Sandra J. Lindow (Menomonie) lives on a hilltop where she transcends pandemic isolation by digging up her vegetable beds and spending quality time with her daffodils. Her most recent poetry chapbook is *The Island of Amazonned Women: A Warrior Woman's Guide to Breast Cancer and Recovery.*

Debra Monthei Manske (South Milwaukee) is a poet who writes from a cluttered upper office. *Peace is Every Step* helped her get started on her second act.

CJ Muchhala (Shorewood) has work appearing in anthologies, art exhibits, and print and online journals, and has been nominated for the Best of Net and Pushcart prizes.

C. L. Nehmer (Brookfield) is the author of *The Alchemy of Planes: Amelia Earhart's Life in Verse.* Her work has appeared in *Southern Poetry Review, Pedestal Magazine,* and other journals. *www.clnehmer.com*

Elizabeth Harmatys Park (Burlington) is a prize-winning poet who writes with Authors Echo in Burlington. Her poetry has been published in journals, anthologies, and the *Wisconsin Poets' Calendar.*

June G. Paul (Portage) has a master's degree in religious studies. She has published two books and some of her poems have been published in online lit mags, journals, and reviews.

Ann M. Penton (Green Valley, Arizona; formerly northwestern Wisconsin) has many published poems, including in multiple *Wisconsin Poets' Calendars* and in *Museletter, Bramble*, and Haiku Society of America's Members' Anthologies.

Mary Louise Peters (Madison), a Rhinelander native, found poetry at Rhinelander High School, picks up words and strings them together, writes for work and play (educational consultant/facilitator, poet, grandmother, and aspiring artist).

Karyn Powers (Wausau) lives in central Wisconsin in a 1927 cottage with her husband and two Labs.

Deborah Rasmussen (Duluth, Minnesota) finds peace in nature, in friendship, in the acts of kindness, small and large, that surround us and, of course, in poetry.

Georgia Ressmeyer (Sheboygan) is the author of a chapbook and two full-length poetry books. Her most recent is *Home/Body* (Pebblebrook Press, 2017). *www.georgiaressmeyer.com*

Patricia McNamee Rosenberg (Burlington) moved to Brown's Lake, Wisconsin after the passing of her husband, and found her inner peace by writing again. She is a humorist, poet, and storyteller.

Sara Sarna (Oconomowoc) is a poet and actor in southeastern Wisconsin. Her poetry has appeared in print, online, and on stage. To support her artistic habits, she works in Patient Services.

Jo Scheder (Madison) explores poetry as alternative ethnography, following a career as an anthropologist. Her poems appear in *Poets to Come: A Celebration of Walt Whitman's Bicentennial, Bards Against Hunger Anthology, Verse Wisconsin,* and *Poetry Hall Chinese and English Bilingual Journal.*

Paula Schulz (Slinger) taught for twenty years in grades 3K through college. She loved her time in Africa, where she helped with the preschool students.

Kent Shifferd, Ph.D. (Minong) is a writer living on a small lake in the woods of northwest Wisconsin. He is the author of *From War to Peace* and a new book, *Understanding and Responding to Our Global Crisis,* coming out this spring. He publishes the monthly *Creation Care Newsletter.*

Marshall Smith (Pleasant Prairie) studied in the University of Iowa Writers Workshop MFA Poetry program. He is published in *Soundings,* a poetry anthology, and teaches a selective poetry workshop for Kenosha Writers Guild.

Gail Sosinsky (Madison) is a northern Wisconsin native. She has published both short stories and poetry and is currently revising her first novel.

Elaine Strite (Harshaw) spent nearly three decades in the Middle East. She now lives on a trout stream where the natural landscape and its denizens are a beloved muse.

Thomas A. Thrun (Oconomowoc) holds a B.A in English/Journalism from UW-Platteville, served as editor of a campus newspaper and literary publication, and was a weekly newspaper editor for 10 years. He is a writer inspired by Robert Frost.

Elizabeth Tornes' (Lac du Flambeau) poetry collections include *Snowbound, New Moon,* and *Between the Dog and the Wolf.* Her poems have appeared widely in journals and anthologies.

Peggy Trojan (Brule) published her first poem at age seventy-seven. Since then she has authored three chapbooks and two full-length collections. Her latest is *All That Matters: Collected Poems 2010 – 2018.*

Jenny Tumas (Bayfield) teaches yoga and Introduction to Sanskrit, has studied English and Russian, worked as a proofreader and editor, and loves living immersed in the beauty of northern Wisconsin.

Sue Twiggs (Marshfield) draws inspiration from Wisconsin's woods and lakes and the Arizona desert. She remains grounded by her daily meditation and yoga practice.

Lucy Tyrrell (Bayfield) lived in Alaska for 16 years, but in 2016 traded a big mountain (Denali) for a big lake (Superior). Her favorite verbs to live by are *experience* and *create.* She is Bayfield's Poet Laureate 2020 – 2021.

B. D. Vess (Madison) is a partner, counselor, and father of two. He writes out of a search for hope, beauty, and connection in the ugliness of life.

37044310R00038